Investing in Paradise
The Definitive Guide to Investing in Real Estate in Barbados

Crane Beach, St. Philip

Investing in Paradise
The Definitive Guide to Buying Property in Barbados

By Suzanne Davis

with Daphne Ewing-Chow

First Edition
2017

Copyright © 2017 by Suzanne Davis

All rights reserved. This book or any portion thereof may not be reproduced or used in any manner whatsoever without the express written permission of the author except for the use of brief quotations in a book review or scholarly journal.

First Printing: 2017

ISBN-13: 978-1973205180

www.luxecaribbeanproperties.com

Dedication

To my husband, Ron.

Thank you. Without your support and patience, I would have never achieved my dreams.

Contents

Suzanne Davis: A Biographical Note 2

Barbados: Gem of the Caribbean 12

Reasons for Coming Here 34

Reasons for Investing 44

Tips for Purchasing Property in Barbados 52

Selecting a Real Estate Agent 56

Financial Advice 58

Legal Advice 64

Conclusion 79

Acknowledgements

I want to thank Camilita and Andrew Nuttall who pushed, prodded and eventually pushed me over the edge to write this book.

Also, to Ron, my loving husband who has supported me in my old and now my new ventures.

Thank you to Daphne Ewing-Chow, the writer who was my sidekick and friend during this project.

Thanks also to all those who contributed information, in particular, Dustin Dalany of Delany Law, Savitri St. John of Clarke, Gittens and Farmer and Anita Ashton of Caribbean Mortgage Brokers, it was greatly appreciated!

Suzanne Davis: A Biographical Note

By Daphne Ewing-Chow

I first met Suzanne Davis at a location of our mutual choosing— a little restaurant, free of airs but known for its delicious food. After prolonged rumination over our very selective menu decisions, we each disclosed that we were on somewhat of a "health kick" and were "trying to be good". Suzanne and I would quickly learn that we were seeing the same naturopath, which I suppose is not uncommon on a small island, but upon further discussion, we began to realize just how much we had in common. It soon became apparent that for me, this was not going to be a typical client relationship.

From the start, Suzanne was shy and sweet and soft spoken— and yet convicted— I definitely got the impression that she knew what she was about, what she wanted to achieve and had a strong command of her abilities and the scope of her knowledge. She was also endearingly unguarded about her limitations and vulnerabilities. By our second meeting, Suzanne and I were sharing embarrassing details about our lives and by our third encounter she had already seen me cry. It was at that meeting that I knew for sure that Suzanne and I were going to be very close.

Suzanne was born in Barbados about a decade before luxury real estate was a "thing" on the tropical isle. The famous Sandy Lane Estate and Golf Course would not be developed for another few years, and the majestic homes of this period were primarily old plantation houses that were constructed during the early years of slavery when sugar was the primary economic driver in the small islands of the region.

Suzanne's early years were spent on the property of Applewaite's Plantation, which was managed by her grandparents, Barty and Clare Watson. She was the eldest of four children, followed by siblings, Richard, who was three years her junior, and Geoffrey and Sandra who would be born five and eight years later. The estate was a dream setting for any young child— Suzanne fondly recalls the colourful gardens and the traditional furniture, which was constructed from the Mahogany trees on the property and currently stands in her family home in St. George.

In 1962, professional oil piping projects would take the Browne family to Trinidad, where they would reside for almost a decade. Over the years, they would grow from a family of four to a family of six, with the addition of Geoffrey and Sandra.

Suzanne's parents, Richard and Jean Browne, were in the deep-sea diving business and were involved in various ocean construction projects. Richard did the diving, and Jean managed the office. Richard had a profound love and respect for the ocean, which he would pass on to his children— Suzanne remembers visiting her grand-parents in Barbados and spending holidays at The Powell Spring Hotel on the rustic East Coast of Barbados, Bathsheba, where she would play in shallow pools and soak up the warm sun as a natural cure for her frequent asthma attacks.

As in Barbados, the ocean would play a significant role in the life of the Browne family. Suzanne remembers spending weekends on the beaches of Mayaro and Maracas in Trinidad where she would relax on the shore with her parents, enjoying the social, cultural and environmental diversity that was so different from Barbados and the other islands in the Eastern Caribbean. Suzanne's parents also joined the Yacht Club where they would socialize with other families.

The Browne family were devout Catholics and Suzanne would attend the St. Raphael and St. Joseph Convents. On Sundays the family would attend church and stop at the neighbourhood bakery on the way home, "to get hops and salt prunes," Suzanne fondly remembers.

In her thirteenth year, Suzanne's family relocated to Barbados and she would enrol at the St. Ursuline Convent. The Barbados to which she returned was newly independent and trying to reduce its reliance on the sugar trade. Developers were focusing on the construction of new hotels in response to the growing tourism industry and visitors were arriving to Barbados from Canada and the United Kingdom. foreign companies were also becoming increasingly interested in investing in the rapidly expanding island-economy.

Middle income neighbourhoods such as Heywoods in St. Peter, Sunset Crest in St. James and Rockley Resort in Christ Church were beginning to appear on the landscape and the Barbados Estate Agents and Valuers Association (BEAVA) was established by valuers seeking to meet the increasing demands of the rapidly developing industry; BEAVA members were encouraged to adhere to a code of ethics and standards. This would one day become one of Suzanne's primary objectives as a leader and visionary in the local real estate industry.

Upon their relocation to Barbados, the family settled on the property of Gibbons Plantation in the parish of Christ Church, where they would reside until Suzanne became an adult. "My favourite spot at Gibbons was the tamarind tree," Suzanne remembers. "Although my asthma prevented me from being athletic, I loved to climb trees. I'd climb up there and I'd look at the world. I was extremely young, but I still remember that those boughs were the first spot where I'd think about the type of man that I wanted to marry— someone who was strong— I'll never forget."

The grounds of the old home provided an aesthetically and spiritually idyllic setting and the young Suzanne would find herself most at home in nature, where she could be surrounded by colour and engaged with the beauty of her surroundings and the old windmill in the distance.

"I have always loved beautiful things," smiles Suzanne. "Perhaps given my history living on the property of old plantation homes, I have developed an appreciation for traditional colonial-Caribbean architecture, set against picturesque gardens."

In more recent years, Suzanne would begin to cultivate an appreciation for the modern North American and European real estate influences that would emerge on the architectural landscape, beautifully complementing the colonial structures to which she was traditionally inclined.

Since its independence, Barbados had rapidly evolved into an upper-middle-income economy and in 1975, the newly formed Central Bank would peg the Barbados dollar exchange rate with that of the United States dollar. These were critical developments in the economic history of Barbados, and the strategic timing of Suzanne's relocation to her birth country as a teen put her in the right place at the right time. In the years into adulthood, the intellectually curious and ambitious adolescent would learn more about business and reflect on her future aspirations— making her somewhat of a renegade for a girl of that period.

Suzanne Davis

"I was never satisfied with where I was," Suzanne laughs. "I was always looking at the next prospect." Her out of the box and curious approach to life would attract her to just the right people, opportunities and experiences, which would continue to be a theme into adulthood.

At the age of 15, unbeknownst to her at the time, Suzanne had a brush with her destiny. On a lazy weekend on the Barbados East Coast, she would lock eyes with the handsome and charming Ronald (Ron) Davis, who was four years her senior and girlfriend at his side. A year later, he would crash her sixteenth birthday party, and he later admitted to Suzanne that he had made up his mind that she "was going to be his girlfriend."

The shy but ambitious Suzanne found her perfect complement in Ron— he supported and encouraged her, while assuming the traditional male role as protector— just as she had envisioned as a young girl. Several years later, in Suzanne's nineteenth year, the couple wed at St. Patrick's Roman Catholic Church before a large congregation of friends and family.

In 1978, six months after their nuptials, the couple moved to Canada with the strategic intention of retaining the Canadian citizenship that Suzanne had acquired through her father, who was born in Canada. Suzanne would arrive three months earlier than her husband so that she could begin her job search and set up a home for the couple, while Ron handled business in Barbados. "It was my first time on my own, and my first time alone," Suzanne remembers. "To be out job hunting in a new country was very unusual for a young woman during those days, but it made me stronger and it gave me skills that continue to benefit me to this day." Suzanne was initially employed by a Japanese firm and then a Canadian Bank.

Suzanne's parents and siblings would follow close behind them, relocating to Canada several years later, and her sister who was eight-years her junior would move in with the couple and enrol at a nearby school. Suzanne and Ron's daughter, Tanya would be born during this period, followed by their second daughter, Christine, four and a half years later.

Motherhood was a role that Suzanne embraced wholeheartedly. "I remember the first time I saw my first child," Suzanne reflects. "I held her perfect head in my hands and was overcome with emotion."

The new mother also struggled with the typical challenges of finding a work-life balance. "I wanted to be home all of the time, but I also wanted to work and I wanted my independence."

Ron would pursue a career in finance with the Canadian branch of the Barbadian bank with which he was previously employed and the couple would become highly active in the multi-level sales and personal development program, Amway, from which they benefited greatly.

"My greatest takeaways from Amway were public speaking and sales. Ron and I are both dreamers and the aspirational value of the program appealed to us both," says Suzanne, who remembers driving through beautiful neighbourhoods on the outskirts of Toronto where they would look at the beautiful homes and dream of their future.

In the latter part of the 1980's, homesickness would entice the Browne and Davis families back home. Suzanne and Ron would buy and renovate his family home and live there for some years until they sold it and relocated to St. George, where they continue to live today. The couple's son, Brent, would be born several years after their relocation to Barbados.

Tanya was enrolled at St. Angela's Roman Catholic School, and later, when she discovered that there was no place she could send Christine, who was a special needs child, Suzanne would spearhead the Special Needs Class at St. Angela's. A second Special Needs Class was then opened in the High School, St Ursula's. Suzanne became very involved with the Parent Teacher's Association and also served as president.

After comfortably resettling in Barbados, the Davis family would spend most of their leisure time by the ocean at The Barbados Yacht Club, the East coast in particular and, would eventually begin to travel to the Grenadines for idyllic holidays on their family boat.

During this period, things were beginning to change in the Barbados luxury real estate market and the tourism industry was thriving. The Concorde provided a regular service to the island, which was a major draw card for big spenders from the United Kingdom. The highly ambitious Suzanne was determined to make a living for herself and her young family.

Suzanne took a position at a local hotel where she was responsible for the "human" element of the business— coordinating reservations, activities and events. While she enjoyed problem solving and meeting and interacting with people, the family-oriented mother eventually chose to forego the long hours so that she could dedicate more time to her young children.

In 1987 Suzanne was offered a position with a small real estate company, which she accepted— the hours were more manageable and the property market was rapidly developing. Being involved with the business from its early stages gave her the benefit of gaining competency in all areas of Barbados' buzzing real estate business— sales, short and long-term rentals and property management— which was where the money was at, and Suzanne was right in the hub of the activity. As the company grew, Suzanne was promoted to management and eventually became a shareholder in the real estate arm of the business. This coincided with a very lucrative period in the economic history of Barbados, and Suzanne was extremely busy. She became very involved in the management, rental and sales of properties in the prestigious Sandy Lane Estate, among other areas.

"That was a wonderful and exciting time for me," remembers Suzanne. "I fell in love with my country all over again. Real estate gave me the opportunity to see a whole other side of Barbados and with different eyes. I have travelled to many places, and I am confident that Barbados truly is the gem of the Caribbean."

In response to the economic prosperity of the latter part of the 1990's, exclusive developments such as the Port St. Charles Marina, Royal Westmoreland golf resort and Sugar Hill tennis resort were emerging on the booming landscape. The lifestyle and residential focus of these properties, coupled with their hotel-style ambience and shared amenities such as tennis, gyms, golf, boating and spas ushered in a new era for the real estate industry, defined by more diversity and heightened exclusivity for discerning investors. Suzanne's clients included families, investors, expatriates, counts and countesses and lords and ladies. She began to better understand people and their needs and the once shy girl who would dream in the tamarind tree of her parent's home was now a cosmopolitan woman who was passionate about her country, the property market and customer service. Barbados was changing drastically, and so was Suzanne.

In the years to follow, timeshare and lifestyle communities, middle-income condominium projects, gated communities and ultra-exclusive beachfront condominiums would emerge on the real estate landscape. Many Bajans were jumping at the opportunity to invest in this trendy segment of the market.

The rapid development of the 1990's would continue for another decade. Many iconic residences and developments emerged and property values benefited from major appreciation, with coastline properties experiencing more than a 100% increase in value during the ten-year period.

Suzanne provided much needed local leadership during the real estate downturn that affected the global property market between 2008 and 2012. Using her platform as president of the only professional real estate body in Barbados, she advocated for the enforcement of quality and ethical standards for the local real estate industry, working on educational programs for aspiring realtors, writing by-laws and championing legislation, so that the country and its real estate industry would re-emerge from the downturn, stronger than it was before.

Since 2015, the local real estate market has been showing major signs of recovery and prices are once again in a healthy growth pattern. Foreign buyers continue to be actively invested in the local property market and demand for South coast properties currently exceeds supply. The development of uber exclusive beachfront developments such as One Sandy Lane and Port Ferdinand Marina and Luxury Residences and the sale of West Coast beachfront property Four Winds for US $40 million in 2016 are further indications of investor confidence.

Suzanne continues to be a major player in the local property industry. She has served on the executive board of the Barbados Estate Agents and Valuers Association Inc. (BEAVA) for the past twelve years, including two stints as president totalling 7 years, and her three decades-long experience in the industry has provided her with extensive experience developing marketing and sales divisions and managing the long and short-term rental divisions of other industry players. Suzanne has always taken great pride in her personal approach, commitment to customer service and meaningful long-term client-relationships.

Suzanne is currently the Owner and President of Luxe Caribbean Properties Inc., specializing in luxury property sales, long term and holiday rentals, valuation and auctioneering services and advice on expatriate relocation, attorneys, mortgage brokers, property management and rentals.

Luxe Caribbean Properties has an impressive portfolio of luxury beach front villas and exclusive Sandy Lane Estate properties, condominium units and villas at Port St. Charles, Port Ferdinand, St. Peters Bay and The Crane, the gated and golf communities of Apes Hill, Royal Westmorland and Sugar Hill Estates as well as the local market representing land and properties all over Barbados.

Ron has continued to be very supportive of his wife's success as a realtor and has helped her in every way that he can, despite his very active career as head of a local finance company. Suzanne's son Brent attended college and studied Real Estate in Canada and has joined his mother's team of real estate professionals, while daughter Tanya, trained in England and is a well-known local dance teacher, who is married with a young son, and daughter Christine, who has taken after her mother, has immersed herself in the arts.

In 2006, upon leaving St. Ursula's, Christine would become one of the first students at the Schoolhouse for Special Needs, which was opened by Mrs. Yasmin Vlahakis, a Special Needs Teacher from the convent. Suzanne and her husband Ron were very involved in developing the school and eventually, at the suggestion of one of her clients, the couple would consider the feasibility of bringing tribute bands to Barbados to raise funds for the school. Suzanne and Ron presented the idea to the Rotary Club of Barbados, of which Ron is a member and Ron would soon become chairperson of the concert planning committee.

With the continued help of Rotary, a lovely old home on one acre of land was bought to house The School House for Special Needs and a cottage industry for the older students and regular fundraising for the school has become an ongoing project for the couple.

Suzanne has been affiliated with many causes and fundraisers over the years such as Breast Cancer and Wheel Chairs for the Old and disabled and she also assists with the Church Flowers.

Not surprisingly, Suzanne has also developed her proclivity towards the arts, not only as an art enthusiast but also as a practitioner, receiving mentorship and training from popular Bajan artistes, Indrani Whittingham and Tracy Williams. "I love the ocean, sunsets, flowers, dancers and vibrant Caribbean colours," shares Suzanne of her aesthetic inspirations.

Suzanne is a quintessential Caribbean woman with her roots firmly grounded in her birth country of Barbados. A love for country, aesthetic beauty and the arts, as well as a deep passion and appreciation for the secrets, benefits, decision-making and road to ownership of property in Barbados, coupled with some three decades of experience in the industry, made collaborating on this book with Suzanne not only enjoyable, but highly educational and beneficial.

For those who are interested in laying their roots in Barbados, there is no better resource.

Barbados: Gem of the Caribbean

Barbados is well known for having a small island vibe without compromising on stability and security. With its beautiful beaches and idyllic weather, a distinctly British culture with strong Caribbean flavour, world class attractions, amenities and solid infrastructure, coupled with natural beauty and rich indigenous heritage, Barbados' unique history, geography and economy have uniquely positioned it as "the gem of the Caribbean" or what many visitors refer to as "the best of both worlds."

History

The first residents of Barbados were Amerindians: the peaceful Tainos (Arawaks) and the stronger, more aggressive Kalinagos (Caribs) who arrived from Venezuela. It is thought that the Kalinagos drove the Tainos off the island but left it alone themselves by the early 1600's.

Some Amerindians were still on the island when Portuguese sailors arrived around 1537 on their way to Brazil. The sailors named the island "Los Barbados", upon finding trees whose roots resemble beards, aptly named "The Bearded Fig Tree".

When the English Captain John Powell arrived in 1625, he found the island deserted of people and claimed it for King James I of England. Powell returned to England along with his employer, Sir William Courteen, with enthusiastic depictions of the island. In 1627, eighty settlers were sent out to inhabit the island in a location that they named Jamestown, after their King. This area is currently known as Holetown.

In the twenty years that followed, the population of Barbados grew exponentially due to political unrest in England and the influx of slaves from Africa. When the British found that they could make a significant amount of money by cultivating sugar, it would rapidly replace tobacco and cotton as the primary crop on the British colony. A cheap labour source was found in African slaves and by the end of the century, 80 percent of Barbados's 85,000 inhabitants were Africans.

English law and traditions took hold so quickly upon settlement by the British that the colony came to be known as "Little England." The first Parliament was held in 1639, making it the third oldest in the Commonwealth, after the British House of Commons and the Bermuda House of Assembly.

In later years, Barbados moved toward the development of an independent civilization with the emancipation of the slaves in 1834, women's right to vote in 1944 and universal adult right to vote in 1951. With the rise of the two-party system and a cabinet government during the 1950's, Barbados was well prepared for independence which was granted on November 30, 1966.

Barbados is a member of the Commonwealth and continues to maintain ties to the Britain monarch who is represented in Barbados by the Governor General. Barbados has two major political parties, The Barbados Labour Party and the Democratic Labour Party. It is politically stable and the crime rate is quite low.

Population

According to Sir Cliff Richards, "The thing I … love about Barbados is the people. The Bajans have a genuine warmth towards all visitors to the island and the 'Platinum' west coast is filled with Brits and Americans who are all very generous with their hospitality." (Adapted from Simon Seeks, 2015)

Barbadians or Bajans, as they are called, are people born in Barbados or elsewhere who have at least one Barbadian parent and maintain cultural ties to the nation. Bajans have an excellent reputation as caring, creative, intelligent, proud and confident people who live life passionately, even in the face of hardship.

The population of 280,000 people is predominantly black (92.4%) or mixed (3.1%). 2.7% of the population is white and 1.3% South Asian. The remaining 0.4% of the population includes East Asians and Middle Easterners.

Weather & Geography

Barbados is a relatively flat island of 166 square miles and is composed primarily of a coral limestone outcropping of the South American continental shelf that lies in the western Atlantic Ocean, 160 kilometres east of Saint Lucia and 320 kilometres north of Trinidad and the northern coast of South America. The highest point is Mount Hillaby, which is located at 336 kilometres above sea level.

Daytime temperatures in Barbados range between 80 to 85 degrees Fahrenheit (27 – 29 Celsius). The prevailing northeast trade winds make the island consistently cool. The rainy or hurricane season runs from June to October, but given Barbados' location in the island chain, it tends to avoid hurricanes.

Infrastructure

Schooling

Barbados offers government-financed education from nursery to secondary level. School is mandatory from 4 years of age to 16 years of age and the island boasts a literacy rate of 99%.

There are over 100 schools in the primary and secondary sectors. Three private schools take children from ages 3-4 to 16. These are St. Winifred's School, the Ursuline Schools, Lockerbie College and Providence Elementary School. The Codrington School is an International Baccalaureate (IB) World School that is authorized to offer all three of the IB's 'gold standard' educational programs for children from ages 3 to 18. Private Primary Schools not listed above that take children from ages 3-4 to age 11 include St. Gabriel's school and Wills Primary.

Educational institutions at the post-secondary level include The Samuel Jackman Prescod Polytechnic (SJPP), the Barbados Community College (BCC) and the University of the West Indies (UWI) Cave Hill campus as well as international institutions such as The American University of Barbados (AUB) and Washington University of Barbados School of Medicine (WUB).

Health Care

Barbados is considered to have the most modern medical facilities in the Eastern Caribbean.

There are two major hospitals, the government owned Queen Elizabeth Hospital and the privately owned Bayview Hospital. Additionally there are more than 20 well-equipped clinics and a number of experienced medical laboratories offering an extensive variety of fundamental testing services. The island's health care sector offers both private and public health care services.

There are also two major 24-hour private medical centres– Sandy Crest on the West coast and the FMH centre closer to Bridgetown. There is also a well-established dental services division and a cutting edge fertility centre.

The University of the West Indies offers clinical and graduate programmes in medicine.

Postal Service

The Barbados Postal Service (BPS) is a branch of the government. There are 18 post offices across the island. In addition to the local Express Mail Service, the BPS offers international services. There is also a pick-up service for corporate customers and government departments. FedEx, DHL and UPS couriers also operate out of Barbados.

Utilities

Barbados has a reliable utilities infrastructure and rates are among the lowest in the Caribbean.

Electricity

Barbados has a dependable supply of power. The sole provider of power is the Barbados Light and Power Company. The household and business supply voltage is 115/230 volts 50Hz.

Solar power is widely utilized throughout the island for water heaters and is increasingly being used to generate electricity.

Telecommunications

Barbados is furnished with the most current media communications framework in the Eastern Caribbean, with the most recent in computerized innovation and fibre optic systems, global direct dialling and satellite broadcast communications.

The main mobile phone and Internet suppliers are Digicel and Flow (also a landline provider).

Barbados offers global roaming and works under the universally recognized GSM network. The International direct dialling code for Barbados is 1-246, followed by a seven-digit number.

Water

The Barbados Water Authority, a Government statutory corporation, is the sole provider of water services. Water is safe to drink directly from the tap. Monthly bills for water service are based on metered usage.

Banking

Barbados has a modern banking system with a variety of commercial banks in operation, including indigenous (RBTT, Republic, First Citizens, CIBC First Caribbean International Bank) and international banks (Scotiabank, Royal Bank of Canada).

Most banks offer a number of branches and a typical range of personal and business services and ATM's.

Airport and Accessibility

The island's only airport, Grantley Adams International Airport (GAIA) offers shops and state of the art facilities to handle its increasing regional and international traffic. At last count the passenger terminal was handling an estimated of approximately 2 million passengers a year.

Barbados is served by many regional and international carriers including: British Airways, Virgin Atlantic, Air Canada, WestJet,

American Airlines, JetBlue, Caribbean Airlines and LIAT. A number of charter airlines also offer seasonal service, such as Thomas Cook Airlines from the United Kingdom.

Religion

More than 95 percent of the population of Barbados is considered Christian, though many are non-denominational with Anglicanism constituting the largest religious grouping.

There are over 100 other religious affiliations represented in Barbados, each with their own locations of worship. These include Buddhist, Church of Christ, Evangelical, Hindu, Jehovah's Witness, Jewish, Methodist, Moravian, Mormon, Muslim, Pentecostal, Quaker, Roman Catholic and Seventh Day Adventist.

Seaports

Barbados has an international deep water harbour in Bridgetown and is a port of call for a number of British, European and American cruise lines. The Bridgetown Port is the primary point of entry for seagoing vessels. Passengers of cruise ships and other large vessels must clear customs at this point of entry.

Smaller vessels, such as yachts, may clear customs either at the port in Bridgetown or at the Port St. Charles Marina, located on the West Coast of Barbados, in St. Peter.

Roads and Public Transportation

Barbados has a road system of about 1,475 km of paved roads with an efficient highway system that connects the North and the South of the island.

The state-owned Barbados Transport Board runs an extremely efficient public bus service.

Economy

Barbados has a market-based economy. It is considered to the most developed country in the Eastern Caribbean and enjoys one of the highest per capita incomes in the region. Since independence, the

Barbadian economy has diversified from sugarcane cultivation and related activities to light industry and tourism with about four-fifths of GDP and of exports being attributed to services. Offshore finance and information services are also major foreign exchange earners.

Tourism

Tourism is Barbados' primary economic driver. According to the Barbados Tourism Investment Inc., Barbados is in the top ten for visitor arrivals in the region, and the number one destination in the region for visitors from the UK. It is also number 1 for visitor-spend per capita in the top ten categories and is responsible for over 50% of the country's foreign exchange. According to the Caribbean Tourism Organization, Barbados recorded a 6.7 per cent increase in international visitors in 2016, with a recorded 631,513 stay-over visitors (Barbados Statistical Service). Visitors arrive primarily from the United Kingdom, United States, other Caribbean destinations & Latin America and Canada. Peak season is from mid-December through April.

The Offshore Sector

Barbados enjoys a positive image in the marketplace as a reputable International Business Centre, benefitting from the same time zone as eastern US financial centres, a highly educated workforce, as well as a constantly improving investment climate, and has been successfully attracting Foreign Direct Investment for decades, particularly from North America. Barbados attracted Cdn$70.3 billion and Cdn$79.9 billion of direct investment at the end of 2014 and 2015, making it the 3rd leading destination for Canadian direct investment abroad.

The Real Estate Industry Offering

Barbados is well known for its sophisticated real estate offering and there are a variety of options for discerning investors.

Pundits anticipate further increases in the demand for property, especially amongst the British who account for a significant amount of foreign sales.

Types of Properties

Properties in Barbados include beachfront apartments and condominiums, holiday homes, luxury villas, residential lifestyle communities and family homes. The following are some of the more popular types of properties.

Luxury Villas

Luxury villas have become a popular option for discerning vacationers and property investors. The added privacy, dedicated staff, and bespoke service make this type of property an excellent choice for a vacation or an investment property.

Barbados is also known for its beautiful historic plantation homes with their grand colonial architecture, tall casement windows with wooden shutters and mahogany floors. Plantation homes sit on large estates and are usually in need of some refurbishment, which can be both an enjoyable and worthwhile project, given their authentic beauty and value. Many of these Plantation Homes have sold off the agricultural acreage and maintain just a few acres for gardens and in some cases horse stables and paddocks.

There are a number of luxury villas sprinkled around the island, particularly on the exclusive platinum coast of Barbados. These consist of stand-alone beachfront properties, villas in contained resort communities and homes that are located in exclusive neighbourhoods such as the famous Sandy Lane Estate.

Investing in Paradise: The Definitive Guide to Buying Real Estate in Barbados

Beachfront property, Villa Bonita

    The Sandy Lane Estate: Sandy Lane Estate is the most prestigious address on the island with magnificent villas set in lush one and two acre gardens, built around the Sandy Lane Golf Course. Sandy Lane Estate has private beach facilities for residents and guests, located next to The Sandy Lane Hotel. This community is not gated and is more of a neighbourhood with some shared amenities.

Oriana, Sandy Lane

Residential Lifestyle Communities

Lifestyle communities bring together exclusive living with recreation, dining and wellness. This type of community has become quite trendy in Barbados. The following are examples of some of the more fashionable lifestyle communities in Barbados.

Apes Hill: This is the only Golf, Polo and Tennis Community of Barbados and boasts prime land with panoramic views of the Caribbean Sea, prime land, located some 1,000 feet above sea level. Clients can choose from luxurious villas or town houses already built, or build their own. Amenities include a clubhouse with restaurant, gym and pools.

Sugar Hill Estate: The resort community features communal pools, championship tennis courts, a clubhouse, a health club and a restaurant on site. Many of the properties also have their own private pools. Sir Cliff Richard is an owner here.

Royal Westmoreland: This former sugar cane plantation is a luxury sporting and leisure destination consisting of apartments and luxury villas, a Robert Trent Jones junior designed 18-hole championship golf course, tennis and gym facilities, a spa and beach club, swimming pools and an impressive Colonial-style clubhouse.

Westmoreland Hills: Located in St. James, Westmoreland Hills is one of the newer luxury developments in Barbados and features 2-4 bedroom eco-friendly homes with private amenities such as a fitness centre, a children's play area, pools and a cafe. What is particularly striking about this gated community are the panoramic views that are available from each home.

Westmoreland Hills

Marina Communities

Also catering to the yachting community are Port Ferdinand and Port St Charles.

Port Ferdinand: Port Ferdinand is located near Speightstown in St. Peter and consists of 83 luxury residences and 120 yacht berths in a 16-acre marina community. This is a resort-style community with 5-star service and a variety of amenities and luxuries such as an upscale restaurant, a spa, fitness centre, children's centre and pools.

Port Ferdinand

Port St. Charles: Port St. Charles is located adjacent to Speightstown in St. Peter, and consists of a large lagoon surrounded by one to five bedroom luxury homes and condominiums in a resort-style 22-acre setting. Some amenities include a salon, a yacht club with restaurant, a fitness centre, a marina and pools. The community sits on a beautiful white sandy beach.

Port St. Charles

Beachfront Condominiums

This category of real estate became extremely popular at the turn of the century; properties located on the West or Platinum Coast command the highest prices.

Jerry Steinbok, a well know developer on the island, has built luxury developments such as Beacon Hill Condominiums and Summerland Condominium Villas. He is awaiting additional permissions to construct a condominium hotel investment development, known as Summerland Hotel, as he has decided to add two more floors to the original concept. All of these developments are on the West Coast of Barbados, across from the Beach.

"My first choice is across the road from the beach on the West Coast because the beach land is in short supply and always very expensive and the cost of building is the same no matter where you are building in Barbados. The long term rents for the same product on the West Coast are at least fifty percent higher and the same for short term Tourist Rentals," says Mr. Steinbok.

Some popular beachfront properties include:

One Sandy Lane: One Sandy Lane is the most exclusive beachfront development in Barbados. With eight spacious villas, a tranquil beach, an infinity pool, manicured gardens and a dedicated service team for each villa with a 24-hour concierge, it is not surprising that Rihanna frequently vacations here.

St. Peter's Bay: Located on the beachfront in St. Peter, St. Peter's Bay is a luxury 5-Star condominium development, consisting of two to five bedroom residences and vacation rentals with resort-style services and amenities, such as a spa, restaurant, hair salon, fitness centre and pools.

St. Peter's Bay

The Crane: The Crane is known as "the private residential community within a private resort" and sits on the Southeast coast of Barbados. These consist of two to three-bedroom private residences between 2,000 and 4,000 square feet, on a beautiful resort property and sitting on one of the most beautiful beaches in the world. The Crane also has time-share accommodation.

Some more upscale South coast apartments include Margate Gardens, Palm Beach and Sapphire Beach.

Beauty, Attractions and Culture

From underground caves, to beach vistas and the variety of colourful flora across tropical landscapes, Barbados is abundant in natural beauty. The country's aesthetic charms are beautifully complemented by its laid-back culture and beach lifestyle.

Said Sir Cliff Richard in 2017, "Life doesn't have to pull you here and there. Just think Barbados and it will slow things down for you."

Beaches and Water Sports

The beaches along the Western and Southern coasts border the Caribbean Sea and are thus the most placid. Many of the beaches have public facilities, beach rentals and restaurants. The Eastern side of the island borders the Atlantic and with its more turbulent waves, it is an attraction for surfers. There are no private beaches in Barbados.

Some of the more popular beaches are as follows:

Accra
This south coast beach is a favourite of both tourists and locals. Vendors can be found in kiosks selling clothing and jewellery. Beach-goers can enjoy water sports such as boogie boarding, body surfing, wind surfing and snorkelling.

Accra Beach

Bathsheba
This dramatic East Coast beach buzzes with life when the surf contests come to town. For those who do not surf, there are also pools and reefs ideal for soaking and lying in the sun. The view and scenery are nothing short of a spiritual experience.

Suzanne Davis

Bathsheba beach

Boatyard
The Boatyard offers top-notch beach facilities, a placid ocean and family friendly dining and activities. A beach package is offered at Adventure Beach and includes meals in the seafront restaurant.

Pebbles
Pebbles beach is situated on the south-western coast of Barbados, south of Browne's Beach and north of Needham's Point. With its white sands and turquoise waters, it is a stunning spot for sunbathing and strolling. With its placid swells, it is also an ideal beach for kids.

Mullins
Mullins is a popular hangout with an enchanting bay encompassed by a serene beach, ideal for unwinding. There's a beach bar and an extensive offering of water sports, snorkelling and climbing structures in the water.

Nightlife

Harbour Lights
Harbour Lights is one of the most energetic nightclubs in Barbados and is located on Carlisle Bay Beach. Patrons feast on grilled fish and hamburgers while enjoying DJ music and live cultural entertainment like fire eating, stilt walking and limbo dancing at the Beach Extravaganza Dinner Show.

First and Second Street

Located in Holetown, across the street from Limegrove Lifestyle Centre, First and Second Street feature a horseshoe shaped configuration of bars and restaurants including Indian food, Italian food, Sushi, Chinese food and Caribbean Food. The Trendy Red Door Lounge is a popular nightspot in the area.

St. Lawrence Gap

Located on the South Coast of Barbados, St. Lawrence Gap comes a light at night, offering street food, fine dining, bars and clubs. Two of the more popular clubs in St. Lawrence Gap include the Cove and the Old Jamm Inn. The Cove offers a wide range of music, from reggae, calypso, mellow music and R&B. The Old Jamm Inn offers a wide selection of live and DJ music from jazz to soca.

Historical sites

Barbados Museum and Historical Society

Situated in the UNESCO World Heritage site, Historic Bridgetown and its Garrison, the Barbados Museum and Historical Society is housed in a former 19th century military prison. The building, whose upper area was built in 1818 and lower area in 1853, became the headquarters of the Barbados Museum and Historical Society in 1933.

George Washington House

George Washington, later to become the 1st President of the United States of America, came to Barbados in 1751 and stayed for about two months. George Washington house is the only place George Washington ever stayed outside of the USA.

Nidhe Israel Museum and Synagogue

The Bridgetown Synagogue was built by 1654 and is the oldest synagogue in the Western Hemisphere. The synagogue was damaged by a hurricane in 1831, was repaired, fell into disrepair and was sold to the Hutchinson family in 1929. In 1983, it was saved from destruction by the community and was restored to its present state. Today, the restored synagogue features a museum and walking tour.

Nature/ Eco

Farley Hill Park

An idyllic landscape, set on the grounds of the once majestic Farley Hill house. A manor in ruins, concealed in a forest of mahogany trees, high up on a slope sitting above the tough Atlantic drift, Farley Hill is a perfect spot for picnicking, escaping into nature, covering up in the shade of a consoling tree and gazing out to the ocean.

A few times each year, Farley Hill is transformed into a stage for music festivals.

Harrison's Cave

Harrison's Cave is an enormous underground cave system situated in the focal uplands of Barbados. Its expansive caves and wonderful solidified arrangements make this world-class fascination, the unmatched excellence of the Caribbean and an absolute necessity to see when on vacation.

Harrison's Cave

Hunte's Gardens

Hunte's Gardens, located in St. Joseph is a beautiful arrangement of mini-gardens implanted inside the primary expansive unit, joining dynamic hues and surfaces of uncommon colourful plants to offer a guest the most transcending and captivating experience.

Welchman Hall Gully

Welchman Hall Gully, situated in the parish of St. Thomas, is a three-quarter mile long gully that is home to various tropical plants and trees. It was shaped by the caved in tops of caves, and is still topographically associated with Harrison's Cave.

Sports

Barbados is well known for its sports tourism. Sports offered on a wide scale include tennis, cricket, football and basketball. Other options include golf, car racing, horseracing, polo, martial arts, yoga and water sports.

Golf

Barbados is a golfer's paradise. The island offers two smaller golf courses and several larger luxury golf courses such as Sandy Lane's Green Monkey golf course, the Robert Trent Jones Jr. designed golf course in Royal Westmoreland and the beautiful golf course at the Apes Hill Club.

Apes Hill Club golf course

Polo

Polo is a popular spectator sport for both locals and tourists and has been played in Barbados since 1884. The polo season runs through to May and games are played by international teams to a local home crowd. Polo fields include Apes Hill, Lion Castle and Barbados Polo Club.

Barbados polo

Shopping

Barbados is a duty-free destination for luxury and lifestyle shopping experiences. The following are some more popular picks for shopping in Barbados:

South Coast: Sheraton Mall is Barbados' largest shopping centre with a great deal of diversity in shopping options. Pelican Village is an excellent option for crafts and souvenirs. Lanterns mall is another local mall with a variety of shops.

Bridgetown: Cave Shepherd offers the best in duty free shopping

West Coast: Limegrove Lifestyle Centre, located in Holetown, offers the best in high-end shopping in Barbados. The centre offers designer stores, cafés, bars, restaurants and entertainment. Also on the West Coast are specialty boutiques such as Beth and Tracie, located on the outskirts of Holetown.

Limegrove Lifestyle Centre

Events

In addition to the extensive offering of things to do, Barbados is also home to a large number of local and international events, such as the Sandy Lane Gold Cup, Broadway to Barbados, Holders Season and Grand Kadooment.

Grand Kadooment is Barbados' carnival. Its historical origins go back to the annual festival to celebrate the end of the sugarcane season or "crop over". Colourful costumes, bands and upbeat soca, festivities and dancing in the street make this indigenous event a huge drawcard for locals and tourists alike.

Rihanna at Kadooment

Regular charity events are also highly enjoyable. If visiting Barbados, your concierge or property manager can help you to identify events that occur around the time of your visit.

In addition to a high level of development, a thriving tourism sector and safety and stability, Barbados is abounding with natural beauty. It is the perfect location for couples, families and singles alike and although only 166 square miles in area, it boasts a little bit of something for everyone.

Reasons for Coming Here

"We spent our honeymoon in Barbados in a fabulous rented villa called Benclare ... on what is now the Sandy Lane Estate. It was perched on a hill with a sweeping lawn to the main road, views of the sea and a full staff. One day we were out in the garden and the maid said, 'Oh, look, there's the Queen of England!' Sure enough, there she was, driving past in an open-topped car waving to everyone, with Prince Philip sitting beside her, head buried in a newspaper. We spent beautiful sunny days exploring the island, playing in the sea and having romantic dinners at home to the sound of the ever-present tree frogs. We lounged on the beach, went to the famous Sandy Lane Hotel, swam, talked and walked, and I was so happy I thought I might burst. It was bliss to have George to myself, no work pulling either of us and no fans making life a misery."

- Pattie Harrison, 1966

Pattie Harrison's depiction of her 1966 honeymoon to The Beatles' George Harrison might as well have taken place just yesterday. The beauty, privacy, laissez-faire lifestyle, friendliness and exclusivity that characterized life on the small island more than fifty years ago all continue to make Barbados both endearing and unique to this day.

In 2016, Barbados was ranked as number 4 in Trip Advisor's top islands of the Caribbean, number 4 in U.S. News & World Report's "Best Affordable Caribbean Destinations" (the only island in the Lesser Antilles to make the top 5) and is consistently at the top of world rankings for its beaches and beauty.

What makes Barbados most special— a haven for those who chose to come here— is that which the island makes no effort to achieve— its innate and natural beauty. It is not difficult to see why Thrillist ranked Barbados as the "8th most beautiful island on earth" in 2014.

On the socio-economic front, Barbados is also at the very top of the world rankings. Each year, the World Economic Forum releases its Global Competitiveness Report.

This index is based on the "12 pillars of competitiveness," which include macro-economic environment, infrastructure, health and primary education, and labour market efficiency— Barbados has consistently been on the top of these rankings. Barbados also has the fifth highest Human Development Index in the Americas according to the United Nations[1].

Culturally, Barbados also stands out. Coupled with rich Caribbean cultural elements, such as food, music, and its annual carnival, Barbados is distinctly British; from the first landing of sailors in 1625 until its independence in 1966, Barbados was under uninterrupted British rule— it has certainly earned its nickname of Bimshire or Little England—from the concentration of cricket pitches and polo fields, to the customary teatime enjoyed by many locals, British place names, such as Chancery Lane, Hastings and Scarborough and colonial architecture. Sir Edward Cunard and Ronald Tree, who lived in Barbados in the early twentieth century made a significant contribution to the "Britishness" of Barbados. Cunard, a member of the famous shipping family, acquired the Glitter Bay property in the 1930's and was Winston Churchill's frequent host during the Second World War. In 1946, Cunard rented Glitter Bay to British MP Ronald Tree, who would later go on to develop Sandy Lane Hotel, just around the corner.

According to British horse trainer, Jamie Poulton, "I have been vacationing in Barbados for quite some time. Barbados has always offered me the best of both worlds— beauty and serenity coupled with amazing nightlife and the best in dining. I am currently actively looking to invest in property on the island."

For those looking for swanky bars, polo, golfing, some of the finest dining in the world and ultra-exclusive accommodations (One Sandy Lane apartments peak season rates can surpass $25,000 USD per night), Barbados is the ultra-chic go-to destination for the global who's-who.

Barbados joins Antigua, Canouan Island in the Grenadines and Anguilla as having one of the few global hotels with Leading Hotels of the World status and according to the Telegraph, "No other

---

[1] The Human Development Index (HDI) is a measure of a country's development, and combines a number of indexes: life expectancy, literacy, educational attainment, and GDP per capita for countries worldwide.

Caribbean country can match Barbados for the choice and quality of places to eat out."

The beaches, amenities, shopping, sport and nightlife make Barbados the most bustling and enjoyable island to visit in the region. That, coupled with stability, solid infrastructure and proximity to major ports makes Barbados an obvious option— the Gem of the Caribbean.

People who come to Barbados

Celebrities and High Profile Individuals

One only has to look at the extensive list of celebrities and A-listers who have forged strong connections with the small island over the years for proof of its exclusivity.

Simon Cowell hosts an annual New Year's party here, singer Sir Cliff Richard is a regular on the local party circuit, golfer Tiger Woods, British designer, Erin Fetherstone and British celeb Karen Walsh were all married here, and composer and producer Lord Andrew Lloyd Webber, the Rooneys, Tony Blair, Mark Thatcher (Margaret Thatcher's son) and the Kidds are part of an exclusive club who have or have had a local home-base. It is also the place where Claudette Colbert would come every winter to visit her plantation beachfront home, Bellerive, with friends Frank Sinatra, Babe Paley and Slim Keith.

Both Lord Andrew Lloyd Webber and Sir Cliff Richards have taken an active interest in the development of Barbados. Lord Andrew Lloyd Webber is chair of the island's National Restoration Program and Preservation Trust and Sir Cliff is often in attendance at local charitable events. Lady Lloyd Webber has taken an interest in The School House for Special Needs and pays them a visit each time she is on the island.

Frequent vacationers to Barbados include model Carla Delavigne, Hugh Grant and his former girlfriend Jemima Khan, actress Gwenyth Paltrow, famous-actor-couple Hayden Christensen and Rachel Bilson, Top Gear presenter Chris Evans, singer Kylie Minogue and her sister Danni Minogue, Robert Plant, actor Jude Law and his former girl-friend, actress Sienna Miller, Sir Paul McCartney, Sir Mick Jagger and Prince Harry is a regular visitor to the island.

Many celebrities also have roots in Barbados, the most famous of which is of course, Rihanna. Gwenyth Paltrow, Jada Pinkett-Smith, Mini Driver and LL Cool J also have familial and ancestral connections to the small island.

Celebrities and A-listers claim that the fact that celebrities are generally left alone by the local population is a major draw-card for the small island.

Repeat and Multi-generational Visitors and Vacation-Villa Owners

Barbados boasts an annual-pilgrimage crowd, who seek the winter-sun. According to William "Billy" Griffith, CEO of the Barbados Tourism Marketing Inc. (BTMI), "More tourists are coming to our shores and they are spending more." The 6.7% increase in tourism numbers for 2016 represent a turnaround from the economic slow-down that Barbados experienced in the years between 2012 and 2014. According to a 2014 report from the Atlanta Black Star, at least 18 billionaires own property on the island; some spend a great deal of the year here, including Ottawa Senators owner Eugene Melnyk, who has lived in Barbados since 1991.

"I come to Barbados every year because I know it's the place in the world I can truly relate to and relax, the beautiful people the beautiful scenery and beaches that cleanse my soul," says racehorse trainer, Jamie Poulton.

There are some 90 beachfront villas on the West Coast, with a dozen or so bearing price tags in excess of $50-million US dollars. There are of course neighbourhoods and estates that are not located on the beach front such as Sandy Lane estate, Royal Westmoreland and other resorts that have a great deal of prestige. Among Barbados' illustrious vacation homes are former racehorse owner Robert Sangster's 'Jane's Harbour', Hans Rausing's 'Greensleeves', John Moreton's 'Alegria' and Lord and Lady Bamfords' fabled Heron Bay, which was once owned by Ronald and Marietta Tree.

There are also a number of beachfront condos, villas and townhouses that are located further inland that are used as vacation homes. Sandy Lane Estate, Royal Westmoreland, Sugar Hill, Apes Hill and

Investing in Paradise: The Definitive Guide to Buying Real Estate in Barbados

The Crane have a variety of options for those with more upscale tastes. Owners include Lord Andrew Lloyd Webber, Cilla Black, Wayne Rooney and Sir Cliff Richard.

Owner of Moneysupermarket, Travelsupermarket and SimonEscapes, Simon Nixon selected Barbados as one of a few select locations for his luxury holiday rental company. Nixon spent many years travelling for business "fleeting in and out of hotels", which eventually turned him off of the notion of hotel-centered escapes. Nixon was also interested in investing the wealth that he had accumulated with the success of his internet businesses. These were the catalysts for his investment in properties in the United Kingdom, (Cornwall, the Cotswolds and Cumbria), Spain (Mallorca), the United States (Malibu, California) and the Caribbean (Barbados).

Says Nixon of a typical day at Godings, his 13,500 square foot luxury villa in Barbados, "I love to take a paddle board and make my way over to Mullins and have lunch and then paddle back home. I also love to wake up in the morning and swim over to the platform in the water which is about 150 meters out and then swim back in and have the breakfast that the chef would have prepared for me while I was out."

Lady Olivia Clarke has been travelling to Barbados with her family for the past twenty years, and says "I come here every chance I get."

The Whelan family, Owners of Wigan Athletic, have been coming to Barbados for the past four decades and Dave Whelan has invested millions of dollars into the island, purchasing the Lone Star, one of the most prestigious boutique hotels and restaurants on the island. "This is the island that my wife and I absolutely love. We always think about Barbados," Whelan has said.

The Tabor family who own a $35 million home in Barbados and one-third of the Sandy Lane Hotel also split their time between Barbados and Monaco.

Hans Kristian Rausing, the billionaire legacy son of Swedish packaging titan Hans Rausing owns Greensleeves, an 11-bedroom mansion on the west coast, where he would vacation with his wife Eva before her untimely death in 2012.

According to Jodie Kidd, "Barbados really is THE island to be on… most Britons you see there are those who just regularly visit for their holidays. They have houses here – everyone from the Bamfords to the Rothschilds who used to stay here."

Retirees

The British Expat guide ranked Barbados as one of the world's top ten countries for retirement in 2016. Among the reasons cited were the reliable weather, low risk of hurricanes, excellent healthcare, diversity, the ability to claim foreign pension while living on the island and the natural life of the island.

The Telegraph also recently ranked Barbados as number 4 in its list of the top ten places to retire worldwide, stating "this island member of the Commonwealth has all you would expect from the Caribbean: sun, sea, sand and friendliness. The English language is a huge bonus, although its main selling points include virtually free health care, low property tax, an average temperature of 26C and more than 27,000 British expats to help you feel at home."

Families and business people accompanied by their families

Family life in Barbados is both simple and meaningful. Expatriates have commonly stated their happiness with the lifestyle that their children and families have been able to experience; one that they would not have had the opportunity to enjoy if they had lived else- where.

Collaborative networks are common for those without on-island family-ties and there are various baby and toddler groups for those whose children are not at school age. There is also cheap, honest and efficient support in the form of nannies and cleaning companies— something that is highly uncommon or restrictively expensive in North America and Europe.

Children integrate and interact with peers of all races and cultures and enjoy the benefits of a warm tropical climate, beautiful beaches, and the simplicity of nature— including the regular sites of green monkeys, birds, and extensive vegetation.

Patricia Woods migrated to Barbados in 2006 with her husband Ben, who was the Country Manager of Pricesmart at the time, and their two boys Brandon and Jason. The family lived in Barbados for several years before they relocated to Trinidad on another posting.

"I wouldn't give up that time for anything," Patricia explains of her family's stint in Barbados.

"Our time there was invaluable to my family— we came to appreciate the value of friendships, the beauty of natural living and the simpler things in life, while still benefiting from upscale accommodations, excellent schooling and the opportunity to save some money, given the tax benefits."

The family continues to visit Barbados on holidays.

According to British Journalist, Yvonne Harvey, who produced a blog on her family's experience as expats in Barbados, "This abundant natural beauty has become my backdrop. And it's improved my quality of life considerably since our arrival in August 2013. But there is so much more to this Caribbean nation than meets the eye."

Harvey describes some of the more "taken for granted" benefits of living in Barbados, such as not worrying about arriving late, smiling people who always greet each other and "having your shopping packed into bags and carried to the car every time you visit the supermarket".

Former British High Commissioner, Victoria Dean, who came to Barbados in 2012 with her husband and two children had the opportunity to benefit from Barbados' proximity to other islands in the Eastern Caribbean that also fell under her jurisdiction as High Commissioner.

"Moving to Barbados was an easy decision but one I'm glad we thought hard about as a family. There are wonderful schools on offer, welcoming people and the glorious weather and surroundings," says Victoria of the various benefits of living in Barbados. That said, Victoria's family also experienced a number of teething pains that are typical for migrants.

"Settling in was easy even though we felt that we were in a completely different world to the one we had left behind in Europe, which of course we were! Systems for getting things done in Barbados were certainly different and at times frustratingly slow and bureaucratic. Getting to grips with the roads and navigating a new place with fewer street signs is always an adventure took a while. I was regularly lost and learnt to navigate by pointing myself to the sea! But a smile and politeness goes a very long way here, and people are very willing to help. If you want Island life, with the peace and beauty and beaches that offers, coupled with a rousing social scene, rich cultural life and a warm welcome, as well as an exciting international business opportunity, then I heartily recommend making Barbados the home of your business and your family."

Virtual Offices and Location Independent Professionals

Barbados is a haven for digital nomads; it ranked number 3 in Latin America and the Caribbean for availability of latest technologies in the 2016-2017 Global Competitiveness report and in 2015, it ranked as number 2 in the region for "network readiness", according to the World Economic Forum's Global Information Technology Report which makes it the perfect location for those with virtual offices who seek an escape from the hustle and bustle of urban life.

The island has recently opened its first co-working space where small businesses, freelancers and sole traders can rent spaces, share printers and coffee machines and benefit from administrative support.

Tech-entrepreneurs, Peter Forth and his wife Catherine Komlodi, moved to Barbados to take advantage of the tropical lifestyle that their family could enjoy while still earning a living through their virtual office.

"I'm a serial expat with nine or ten countries under my belt, so it wasn't much of an arm twist when my husband suggested we move to Barbados for a year or two," says Catherine. "We were Canadians living in California at the time, and when our stint in the States was up we jumped at the opportunity to avoid winter for a while longer and have a bit of a beachy adventure while our kids were young. Flash forward twelve years, and we're still here. Something about the laidback lifestyle and friendly community agrees with us, and we haven't felt that itch to leave just yet. We are part of a growing tribe of self-employed "LIPs" (location-independent professionals) and have no desire to jump back into the stress-filled corporate rat race again. Sure, there are petty frustrations that come with island living, but the positives far outweigh the negatives. Our kids have happily grown up here and if we do eventually move on, Barbados will always be home to our family."

Those seeking to make Barbados their Permanent Home

According to the 2017 world rankings from passportindex.com, Barbados has the most powerful passport in the Caribbean and the 50th most powerful in the world. Barbados' passport allows its holders to travel to 132 countries without having to get a visa.

For those who settle down in Barbados, homes tend to be much larger than those in Europe.

Many families have started off as visitors and have returned to make the island their permanent home. A well-known example is the Kidd family from the United Kingdom whose matriarch first visited in 1950, fell in love with the island, and returned several years later to buy the 300-acre Holders House that continues to be the family home.

"My sister Jemma and my mother live here, and every Easter we hold a sort of mini-Glyndebourne in the gardens of the house. It's called the Holders Season and features performances of everything from opera to Shakespeare to mad and wacky musicians and dancers from all over the world," says Jodie Kidd of her family's lifestyle and contribution to Barbados. Holders' house also currently serves as the location of a weekly organic farmer's market.

According to expat, Clare Crew, "Barbados is a beautiful country and there are many reasons one could choose to live here; the beaches, the sunsets, and the culture. For me however, it was the warmth and generosity of the Bajan people that most attracted me. Considering the size of the country, its heart is enormous and nearly everyone here is warm, friendly, embracing and kind. One can always find the odd sort who has a bad attitude, but on the whole, my good experiences have far outweighed the bad. After all, where else can you work, play, live, laugh, sail and swim whenever the whim takes you?"

Paul Doyle, Developer of The Crane Resort moved to Barbados almost 30 years ago and has never looked back.

"I never tire of the amazing lifestyle, beautiful surroundings and hearing the sea, birds and whistling frogs. I'm a very quiet person, but Barbados has something for everyone. Different environments appeal to different people, some prefer the West Coast or maybe the South Coast. Given the lifestyle, a variety of persons are attracted to

Barbados and form communities within communities with very diverse interests. That together with the opportunity to develop in such beautiful surroundings, with big open spaces and turquoise waters, I consider myself very blessed with what we have here in Barbados. The key is Location, Location, Location," he shares.

Barbados certainly has that je ne sais quois, a certain allure that makes it unique and very special. Agatha Christie was so inspired by the island that she used the Coral Reef hotel as a setting for A Caribbean Mystery, which was published in 1964.

Some other unique characteristics that make Barbados different from other countries are little trivialities, such as its title as the birthplace of rum (which has contributed to its thriving rum culture), legend has it that grapefruit originated here, it boasts the oldest synagogue in the Western Hemisphere, it has laid claim to one of the top ten beaches in the world for many years (Crane beach) and has the third oldest parliament in the British Commonwealth.

According to singer, Sir Cliff Richard, "I've been lucky enough to travel the length and breadth of the globe during the course of my music career but whenever I'm asked 'what is your favourite place?' Barbados definitely makes my shortlist."

Reasons for Investing

"I've owned my villa on Barbados for the best part of 10 years now and never grow tired of coming back to escape the British winter! I'd visited the island a few times in the Seventies, Eighties and Nineties and always loved it, so when the opportunity arose for me to have my own secret hideaway on this delightful Caribbean island, I jumped at the chance."

- Sir Cliff Richard

"Of all the Islands, Barbados is the Gem of the Caribbean. That is a fact of life. I have confidence that the market is rebounding and you cannot win the game unless you are in the game."

- Bjorn Bjerkhamn

(Bjorn Bjerkhamn is the developer for Port Ferdinand, St. Peters Bay and was also one of the developers for Port St. Charles. He is currently embarking on another project on the South Coast of the island.)

The Telegraph recently listed Barbados as number five on its top ten places to buy abroad, alongside Lake Como in Italy, Florida, Cote d'Azur in France, the upmarket part of the Western Cape in South Africa and outranking Atlanta, Brussels, Turkey, Berlin and Malta. It was also ranked at number 8 on the Telegraph's list of the world's top ten places to live and has the most powerful passport in the Caribbean and the 50th most powerful in the world.

The property investment story of Sir Cliff Richard, as told to Simon Seeks, is similar to many personal anecdotes of foreigners and expats who have invested in real estate in Barbados, including Andrew Lloyd Weber, the Kidd family, Tony Blair, Manchester United footballer Wayne Rooney and boxer Joe Calzaghe. For those who invest in our island, the welcoming nature of the people and the ease of ownership and doing business make for a strong and effortless emotional connection. In 2017, Sir Cliff Richard received a Barbados Golden Jubilee Award in recognition of his outstanding service to the Barbadian diaspora in the United Kingdom.

Suzanne Davis

According to a recent Wealth-X report, investment properties must combine lifestyle elements such as luxury and amenities, privacy, a strong potential for investment growth and wealth preservation, as well as a 'global gateway' which provides ease of access to international business networks and family. Many of Barbados' luxury properties were developed during the investment boom of the 1960's, when the country was seeking to attract foreign visitors and investment; as a result, the country's investment climate, infrastructure and range of properties were designed with these factors in mind.

As a result, Barbados has a long-standing legal infrastructure for supporting international business. The International Business Companies Act was passed in 1965 and the Society with Restricted Liability Act in 1995.

Barbados has been recognized globally as a destination of choice for investors, and is a highly reputable jurisdiction. This is primarily due to the excellent standard of living and quality of life offered to residents.

Many globally recognized brands have a strong presence here, including the Marriott, the Hilton, Sandals Resorts, Gildan Activewear, Subway, Burger King, Cartier, Michael Kors, Rubis, Colombian Emeralds, Diamonds International, MAC Cosmetics, among others.

Sandals Barbados

Excellent Quality of Life and Solid Infrastructure

Barbados' was ranked 5th in the Americas (and 33rd out of 111 countries) in the Economist Intelligence Unit's Quality of Life Index for 2005 and has one of the lowest poverty rates in the Latin America and Caribbean region. Due to its geographic location, to the left of the

North Atlantic belt, it tends to avoid severe weather, mostly contending with intermittent showers and rare tropical storms during the rainy season. Foreign citizens receive the same legal protections as Barbadian nationals. The legal system and police are unbiased in all matters, commercial and otherwise.

Technologically, Barbados is a highly competitive jurisdiction, coming in second for the Latin America and Caribbean region in the "Networked Readiness Index" World Economic Forum's Global Information Technology Report and 3rd in the region for "availability of latest technology" according to the 2016 Global Competitiveness Report.

Arthur Christopher and his wife Courtney, and their two children moved to Barbados in December of 2016. The couple is in the process of setting up a local business in the medical sector and with the assistance of Luxe Caribbean Properties, they purchased a home on the South Coast of the island.

"I picked Barbados because I knew how solid the infrastructure is as well how stable the economy is, relative to other islands. The government is stable. We knew that we were at minimal risk of being affected by hurricanes. The educational system is great. Our banking relationship has been awesome. We managed to secure a mortgage quickly and easily," attests Christopher.

With highly sophisticated infrastructure and facilities, such as healthcare, education, utilities, technology, transportation and communication, Barbados is on track to achieving its goal of developed nation status by 2025.

Financial Services

The 2016-2017 Global Competitiveness report found Barbados to have the fourth most sound banks in the region and 24th in the world.

Barbados has a well-established financial services ecosystem, which includes banking, advisory services, investment management, wealth management, pensions and other financial services that are highly interconnected with global markets.

Domestically, the financial sector consists of five commercial banks, twelve trust and finance companies and merchant banks and 25 offshore banks. There are also 34 credit unions and two money remitters. International banks, such as Royal Bank of Canada, CIBC (operating as CIBC First Caribbean) and Scotiabank are some of the global banks that have local operations in Barbados. Republic Bank and First Citizens are regional banks with local branches. Each of these banks offer great ease in doing business, which is facilitated by conveniences such as online banking to foreign currency accounts.

Banks are regulated by the Central Bank of Barbados, which also serves as supervisor over the flow of money in and out of the economy, given currency controls. International activities in foreign currencies are not affected by this regime.

Investment managers and fund administrators in Barbados are supervised by the Financial Services Commission.

The International Financial Services Act, which replaced the Offshore Banking Act in June 2002, incorporates Basel standards, and provides for on-site examinations of offshore banks.

Quality of Human Resources

According to the most recent ranking from the United Nations Development Program, Barbados has the fourth highest literacy rate in the world and boasts the 5th highest Human Development Index ranking in the region and number 54 in the world. There are approximately 147,000 Barbadians in the local work force.

The workforce in Barbados is one of the most stable and non-aggressive in the region with rare to no work disruptions.

The skill set in Barbados is highly regarded, due to the high quality of the local values and education. There are a variety of skilled specialists and generalists, and it is very easy to find world-class accountants, lawyers, tax advisors, bankers, realtors and property developers.

Barbados is home to an impressive variety of advisors and investment professionals. The CFA Society of Barbados is an excellent resource for investment professionals and has approximately 50 members, and supports the continuing education of CFA charter holders as well as those pursuing the CFA designation.

Given the quality of human resources and enticing infrastructure, the World Bank has ranked Barbados as one of the top 5 countries in the region for ease of doing business (2016) and number 117 in the world.

Ease of Travel

Grantley Adams International Airport is a world-class airport with over 3,047 m of paved runway handling an estimated 2.3 million passengers a year and offers state of the art facilities to handle its increasing regional and international traffic. The airport receives a large number of daily flights from major international cities including Miami, New York, Toronto, and London, as well as other European countries, countries within Latin America and other islands within the Caribbean region.

Social, Political and Economic Stability and Transparency

Barbados has one of the lowest poverty rates in the world, with steady growth and low inflation and is recognized as having one of the lowest corruption rates in Latin America and in the World.

According to Professor Walid Hejazi,"...the OECD is satisfied that Canadian direct investment abroad that goes to or through Barbados...complies with OECD standards for transparency and exchange of information standards which Barbados expects of all corporations active in its jurisdiction. Conduits like Barbados allow Canadian firms in those industries which drive the global economy to maintain their competitiveness in the global economy." (2007)

Barbados is staunchly committed to its efforts to maintain global standards for foreign investment. According to the OECD's Global Forum, the highest global authority on transparency and the exchange of information for tax purposes, Barbados is the only independent, Caribbean nation that had substantially implemented the internationally agreed tax standard.

Barbados' commitment to compliance and competitiveness is revealed by its 2016 ranking as number 4 for Latin America and the Caribbean in Transparency International's Corruption Perceptions

Index. In 2016 it also ranked as number 9 in the Americas on the Index of Economic Freedom.

Enticing Investment Climate: Mature Jurisdiction with Legal and Financial Incentives

Barbados has one of the most enticing climates for foreign investment in the world. It comes as no surprise that it is the 3rd leading destination for Canadian direct investment abroad, having garnered Cdn$70.3 billion and Cdn$79.9 billion of direct investment from Canada at the end of 2014 and 2015, respectively.

There are no restrictions to buy property on foreign nationals or permanent residents and there are no capital gains or inheritance taxes.

Persons who invest in excess of US$2 Million automatically qualify to apply for a SERP (Special Entry and Residency Permit) towards obtaining residency status in Barbados. (See chapter on legal advice for more information).

High Net Worth Individuals with a net worth of at least US$5 million and who own real estate in Barbados, OR who have made a minimum investment in Barbados of US$2 million (acquired or made with foreign sourced funds) may apply for a Special Entry and Reside Permit (SERP) from the Barbados Immigration Department. Permits may be granted for an indefinite or specified term.

Tax Incentives

Multinational companies use a Barbadian entity to conduct business overseas so as to minimize their global tax burden. Some financial incentives are as follows:

- Low corporate tax rate,
- Exemption from withholding tax on dividends or other income paid to non-residents
- Exemption from taxes on the transfer of certain assets or securities to non-residents
- Freedom from exchange controls.
- No Capital gains tax

- Export allowances with the potential to reduce the effective tax rate to 1.75%.

Barbados' network of double taxation treaties has been rapidly growing, offering tax advantages to investors from partner countries. Tax treaty partners include the economies of "Austria, Bahrain, Botswana, Canada, CARICOM, China, Cuba, the Czech Republic, Finland, Iceland, Luxembourg, Malta, Mauritius, Mexico, the Netherlands, Norway, Panama, Qatar, San Marino, Seychelles, Singapore, Spain, Sweden, Switzerland, the UK, the USA, the United Arab Emirates and Venezuela. Tax treaties with Cyprus, Ghana, Portugal, Italy, Rwanda and Slovak Republic and are awaiting ratification. Barbados has initialled treaties with Belgium, Malaysia and Vietnam. Discussions are ongoing towards the implementation of similar conventions with other nations including Brazil, Chile, and India." (Invest Barbados, 2017)

Price Stability, Ease of Investing in Property and Returns on Real Estate Investment

There are no restrictions for non-nationals to buy real estate in Barbados. Property prices in Barbados are stable and on average show a steady increase in value. Investment in local real estate is a safe source of rental income plus attractive capital appreciation.

"I have continued to invest in Barbados and Royal Westmoreland over the past 12 years because the real estate product is timeless, the UK market knows and trusts Barbados as a high end destination. The high end range of any product never goes out of style," says John Morphet, Owner of Royal Westmoreland.

According to Luxe Caribbean Properties' client Arthur Christopher, "the process of finding and purchasing property, finding the right vendors and making the purchase was as easy or easier than buying a house in the states."

"My wife and I visited Barbados and got to know the island and the neighbourhoods. We narrowed it down to a few neighbourhoods. I went to one of our preferred neighbourhoods and contacted Suzanne. She showed us two homes and we made our decision. Suzanne made the process extremely simple after that. We couldn't be happier."

Companies and individuals looking to thrive in a highly competitive global marketplace invest in Barbados to capitalize on the high quality infrastructure, excellent standard of living, strong human capital, business-friendly environment, tax advantages and investment protection. There is no better location for investment in the region. Perhaps former Secretary-General of the United Nations, Kofi Annan, said it best: Barbados certainly "punches above its weight".

Tips for Purchasing Property in Barbados

Before you start the process of home or property ownership in Barbados, outside of the obvious prerequisite of investment capital, be prepared to embark on an educational, numerical and perhaps even emotional journey. I recommend that you start off by reading this book and then, after establishing some clarity of intent, which includes the purpose for the property, size, area and type of property, start doing your own research and don't be afraid to ask a lot of questions.

The following is a basic "cheat sheet" on the sales process and some considerations and tools to get the investment process off on the right foot.

1. Arrange your finances. Make a decision on what you can comfortably afford. If you will require financing, make sure that you consider the fees and interest for a mortgage. If you need a mortgage, visit your bank or financial institution and determine the best price range for your needs and budget. Make sure to be pre-approved for the maximum number in this range.

2. Find a reputable agent. **You do not need more than one real estate agent.** Your agent should be your partner from the beginning to the end of your real estate journey. In the Barbadian context, the agent that you select should be a recognized, approved agent of the Barbados Estate Agents and Valuers Association. To find the list of approved agents, you can visit www.beavainc.com.

   All BEAVA agents co-broke each other's properties and therefore, they can offer you whatever is listed by other BEAVA agents. It is less stressful for you to deal with one agent who you feel comfortable with and trust, rather than working with several agents who may be showing you properties that you have already seen with another agent.

The right real estate agent will help you do the following in a timely and efficient way:

- Find the right place to fit your budget
- Provide helpful information about Barbados including information on neighbourhoods, security, infrastructure and schools as well as more technical information.
- Answer all questions pertaining to real estate
- Negotiate with sellers, so that you can get a fair price that fits your budget. Offers should be made to sellers on your behalf
- Represent your needs

3. Either independently or with the support of your agent, take time to carefully consider what type of property you like, need and can afford. The location, number of bedrooms and amenities are critical considerations. Also consider whether you might want to purchase a stand-alone villa, a town house or a condominium. Consider the type of neighbourhood that you would like and whether you would like a resort or gated community.

4. Determine how you would like to use the property— will it be an investment property? Your holiday home or will you be staying in it long term? If it is for investment, will you be trying to flip it or will you be using it for short or long-term rentals? Will it remain empty when you are not staying in it?

5. When you have found a property of interest, you will need to ask your agent the following questions:

- Does this property meet my needs; i.e., can I rent it short term/ long term?

- Can I have animals?
- Is this house suitable for children?
- Can I operate a business from the property?
- Are there any concerns about this property?
- Does the property require a structural survey?
- What is a fair price for this property?
- What is the initial offer that I should make?

6. You will need to hire an attorney who is a member of the Bar Association. Your agent will be able to recommend 2 or 3 attorneys who they have previously done business with and can vouch for their reputation and their track record for closing sales in a timely manner.

7. Once the negotiations are complete and a price has been agreed to between the purchaser and vendor, an offer document will be provided by the agent to the purchaser who will complete the document with the required information, which will include but not be limited to the following: name(s) of the purchaser(s) or company purchasing, address and director(s) if it is in a company name, the price of the property with any provisions and a signature. The Offer document will be forwarded to the vendor, who will sign as having accepted the offer. Two pieces of ID and proof of address are required for the Agents records, as is the law in Barbados

8. The signed offer document is included with the agent's instruction letter to the vendor's attorney.

9. The vendor's attorney will draw up a contract and provide it to the purchaser's attorney who will vet the contract, discuss it with the purchaser, decide on a closing date and make any necessary changes.

10. The contract is returned to the vendor's attorney who will vet the changes and discuss with the vendor. When both parties agree with the contract, it is signed by both the vendor and the purchaser and a 10% deposit is paid to the purchaser's attorney.

11. Both attorneys are required to conduct due diligence on the property and financial records should the property be owned by a company. Once everything is in order, the balance of all monies owed will be paid to close the sale. All foreign transactions are recorded by Central Bank in the name of the purchaser. The landmarks are pointed out by a land surveyor to the purchaser or the agent acting on behalf of the purchaser. The keys are then handed to the purchaser or their representative.

Other tips

1. Don't decide based on a photo alone. Make sure to schedule a trip to Barbados and see the property that looks appealing online or on paper.
2. If you are considering building, note that building is not always cheaper than buying or renovating.
3. When factoring in costs, consider the services of a good property manager, especially if you do not plan on living in Barbados full time.
4. Do not exceed your budget. In a worst-case scenario, you can start small and renovate over time.

Selecting a Real Estate Agent

If you have bought this book and reviewed the first few chapters, you are well on your way towards making your dream a reality. The next step is to find someone to help guide you on your journey. Finding and choosing a real estate agent is a big decision, and it can be especially difficult when making a selection from another country.

Despite the temptation, do not select more than one real estate agent. It is logistically confusing and inefficient to use more than one. Any listings that appear for one agent can be shown by any other agent so there is no need for multiple agents.

Use the following process to select a reputable realtor in Barbados:

Go on the Barbados Estate Agents and Valuers Association website (www.beavainc.com). Here you will find a list of all the registered real estate agents in Barbados. BEAVA is the governing body for the real estate industry in Barbados. According to the body, "registered agents who have met the qualifications.... and these agents are bound by the duties imposed by its Code of Ethics. It is the duty of the real estate agent or valuer that he/she be well informed of current market listings and conditions to advise his/her client on the best properties to view that would meet their criteria or the fair market price to list their property."

Visit the websites of the real estate companies to view their inventories and get a feel for the company and the agents who work for them. You can then narrow down your list to no more than three.

You can then contact the Agencies with any queries you may have and if you are planning on visiting Barbados soon, set up appointments to view the properties. The agency will probably suggest other similar properties to view. An experienced Agent should be able to answer your questions and be able to recommend other professionals in the industry such as Attorneys Financial Brokers or Institutions— these are merely suggestions.

Ultimately, experience within the real estate industry and providing the type of services that you are looking for should be a deciding factor. That coupled with an extensive search and a focus on responsiveness and personalized attention make for an effective selection process.

Property Management

Should you be one of the fortunate people who wish to buy a holiday villa or condominium, you will have the choice of having the property managed and rented by one of the experienced Real Estate/Villa Rental Companies on the island. More than likely, the agent who sells you the property also does Property Management and Holiday Rentals. This is a very good idea, as you can feel confident when you are not on island, that your property is in good hands and should you wish to rent, when you are not in residence, they would see after this aspect as well. There will be a monthly management fee which will be decided between you and the Management Company and the maximum rental commission will be 30% depending on the origin of the booking and if there is an overseas agent involved.

Financial Advice

Barbados boasts some of the most lavish luxury properties in the Caribbean region with a wide range of styles and prices that are suitable to various tastes and budgets. An inviting investment climate with no restrictions on property investment for non-nationals, and no property transfer tax for the purchaser or capital gains tax makes Barbados an excellent location for investing in property.

The cost of real estate in Barbados is influenced by neighbourhood and parish/ coast, type of property and community, configuration of the property and whether it is beachfront. For example, a town house in the luxurious Royal Westmoreland community can range from US
$600,000 to US $1,300,000 while a town house in an exclusive community on the South Coast can range from US $350,000 to US $500,000.

Building costs can range anywhere from US$100 per sq. ft. going up to US$500 or more for the luxury segment of the market.

With regards to transaction fees, purchasers can expect to incur attorney fees ranging between 1% – 2% (see chapter on legal advice) plus 17.5% VAT as well as a proportionate amount of land tax. Purchasers are not required to pay property transfer tax but incur 1% stamp duty. The vendor is obligated to pay 2.5% transfer tax (unless the house is registered in the name of an offshore company) and 1% stamp duty their attorney's fees and agent commission.

Annual costs include Property Insurance (US$2.50 to US$3.25 per US$500), Land tax (capped at a maximum of US$30,000 on residences) and Contents Insurance (US$3.00 to US$3.00 per US$500).

Monthly costs include basic utilities such as electricity, water, telephone and cable, pool and garden maintenance, staff, if required, and property management fees.

Property Managers who offer short-term rentals will also charge a commission based on the origination of the booking but will not exceed 30%.

Mortgage considerations for Non-Residents

1. Barbados' mortgage sector can be conservative.
2. Not all local banks offer mortgages to foreigners,
3. Non-resident mortgages are only available in foreign currencies and thus need to be approved by the Central Bank of Barbados which is generally a very straightforward process.
4. Mortgage applicants must also procure a valuation report by one of the approved valuers for that financial institution (see guide below).
5. An attorney is required to complete the purchase process.
6. Repayment terms are between **15 and 20 years** and vary by lender.
7. Mortgages are available according to the following terms
   - 70% LTV up to US$2.5m
   - 60% LTV – US$2.5m to US$5m
   - 50% in excess of US$5m
8. It is extremely useful to secure the advice of a professional mortgage broker

Seeking Advice from a Professional Mortgage Broker
Anita Ashton

A lot has happened in the past 10 years in the Barbados Mortgage market; terms and conditions are much tighter and there is a more diligent lending regime, and cautious lending culture, but in many ways, this is good for both the lenders and the borrowers to ensure they do not over stretch themselves. Borrowing in Barbados is not that much different nowadays from the rest of the world as everyone has tightened up on their terms and conditions.

Seeking a new loan in the current era highlights the importance of enlisting a Professional Mortgage Broker especially when seeking an overseas loan. Each lender has their own criteria and as mortgage brokers it is our job to ensure that you are placed with the right bank for your individual needs.

There are a few lenders in Barbados prepared to offer a non-resident mortgage product. The application needs to be high quality, well presented and meet the terms and conditions of the lender as opposed to the applicant. Employing a mortgage broker who can assist you with this is money well spent.

We don't live in the past, but we can learn from it, lenders will require more scrutiny and income verification from tax authorities. It will take 1 to 3 months to obtain an offer depending on the complexity of the application. Lenders will not process the application until all the documentation is available so you need to be proactive to assist the broker.

A good Mortgage broker can take the hassle and stress from the purchase process and should be engaged early in the buying process. The broker can guide a potential buyer on what might be available in the mortgage funding and if they don't qualify they will l save the purchaser a lot of time and unnecessary stress by informing them up-front. The Barbados mortgage market involves comprehensive scrutiny but we can make the process a smooth operation. We will advise and be the point of contact from other parties to ensure the process is as stress free as possible. Securing real estate in Barbados is an entry into a completely new life style that you will enjoy!

Suzanne Davis

General Information for non-Caribbean Residents

The basic processing of a mortgage application in the Caribbean is similar to many other countries. An Attorney is required and it is advised that all monies are paid through the Attorney, including deposits and mortgage funds received. Normally US$ has the best rates, but the lender can quote for terms. The interest rate is aligned to the US$ 3-months LIBOR rate or US$ Prime depending on the lender. Most loans are on a capital and interest repayment basis and fixed rate loans are available in the region of 3-5 years. However, the interest rate may be higher so demand is low.

In addition, the mortgage is generally limited to 60-65% Loan to value and max 50% to new building with a max term of 15 years.

For those residents of Barbados, a Mortgage Broker can give you the same assistance but your terms and conditions vary to those of non-resident

General Information for Local Mortgages

Local borrowers receive preferential terms and conditions and the reason is simple. Banks and other lenders can obtain all the information at source. The basic Terms and Conditions are:

- The maximum repayment terms is 30 years, with a general age limit of 70
- The lenders can charge a 0-1% arrangement fee
- Loan-to-value can be up to 100%, but 90-95% is more common
- Current interest rates vary so best to get quoted from a Mortgage Broker

Application Checklist

1. Completed Mortgage Application form
2. Employer's letter stating position, salary and length of service or from an Accountant/Company Secretary's letter if self-employed
3. Last three pay slips if applicable

4. Copies of last six months bank statements
5. Photo ID (Barbados ID card preferred)
6. Rent reference if currently renting property
7. Verification of savings/investments
8. Copies of last three annual tax returns
9. Copy of sale agreement (may come direct from attorney)
10. Valuation Report on the property (can follow if approved in principle)
11. Name of Attorney

There are some recent product offerings from the banks, making borrowing in Barbados much more attractive than ever before.

Anita Ashton is the Managing Director of Caribbean Mortgage Services and has over 30 years' experience in UK and Caribbean Banking. She has placed numerous loans for non-residents purchasing in the Caribbean region and is based in Barbados. She can be contacted by telephone at 246 230 5824 or by email at anita@caribbeanmortgages.com

Valuation of a Property

Financial Institutions will require the property to be valued before a mortgage can be approved. There will be a list of recommended valuers used by that institution. The Barbados Estate Agents and Valuers Association website has a list of property valuers.

For land or residential properties, a residential valuer is recommended. However, for a commercial property, it is recommended that a valuer with a professional designation be used.

Legal Advice

Legal counsel is a prerequisite for property investment and development in Barbados. Your real estate agent will provide you with several options for an attorney who is a member of the Bar Association and who will be responsible for reviewing the contract for sale and purchase to ensure that there are no covenants that may hinder future property development. Legal services take about 90-days on average, once there are no extenuating circumstances that may delay completion.

The purchaser is required to pay his or her attorney's legal fees that consist of fixed fees as well as fees that are calculated as a percentage of the value of the sale agreement.

Whether you are a non-national or permanent resident, there are no restrictions on the purchase of property in Barbados. All investors are treated the same in terms of taxation and transaction costs in property transfers.

The remainder of this chapter consists of legal advice from two of the most reputable lawyers in Barbados. The first section is written by Savitri St. John, a Partner with the law firm, Clarke Gittens Farmer and provides a logistical outline, from a legal perspective, on purchasing property. The second section is written by Dustin Delany, Principal of Delany Law and provides an overview of the Special Entry and Reside Permit, which is of particular interest to many foreigners who wish to invest in property and reside locally.

Suzanne Davis

Barbados: Owning a Piece of the Rock, Legal Considerations
Savitri St. John, Partner, Clarke Gittens Farmer

Financing

As with any other purchase, it's important to have a realistic budget.

Residents

How will you finance the purchase?

Many banks will "pre-qualify" you for a loan so you know what you can afford. Remember the cost of buying property includes add-ons like legal fees and taxes, insurances, the cost of repairs and moving costs.

Ask your lawyer early for a ballpark estimate of the fees and expenses on a property within your price range. The legal fees are calculated according to a legislated minimum scale based on the size of your transaction, which you can ask to see.

Taxes include:
- Stamp duty on a mortgage at $3.00 for every $500.00 borrowed
- Duty on other collateral security like life insurance policy assignments and guarantees
- A small fee for recording documents at the Land Registry

If you are borrowing you should also budget for the cost of life and mortgage indemnity insurances that you may be asked to assign to the lender, and for property insurance which will you would need anyway, and which will also have to be assigned.

There are also fees for any expert you hire to inspect the property before you buy it.

Non-residents

You are a non-resident of Barbados if you have not lived in Barbados continuously for the last 3 years, even if you are Barbadian.

Non-residents who are not Barbadian citizens probably won't be permitted to borrow locally to finance the purchase. Make plans to source the funds overseas and send them to Barbados in foreign currency. In the alternative, some banks do offer offshore mortgages to non-residents, in foreign currency. You would need to be resident overseas, and show a foreign currency income stream earned overseas to qualify, among other things.

When foreign currency arrives in Barbados it should be registered with the Exchange Control Authority of the Central Bank of Barbados and will be converted to Barbados Dollars to pay the vendor.

Registration of foreign currency assures you that if and when you wish to repatriate your investment, your request to do so will be entertained by the Exchange Control Authority.

Importation and registration of the foreign currency will probably be a pre-condition for getting permission from the Exchange Control Authority to purchase real estate in Barbados as a non-resident. Evidence that you have been approved for an offshore mortgage would also satisfy the Exchange Control Authority.

When you sell, you will need to apply again to the Exchange Control Authority to do so, but where permission was granted for the initial purchase this is a formality your lawyer will attend to it in the background.

Investors

The rules for overseas investors on local borrowing and importation and export of foreign exchange may be more flexible, depending on the size of the investment, whether you have local partners and (where you are developing real estate for onward sale or rental) your target market for the product.

You will therefore need legal advice tailored to your particular investment.

In particular, bear in mind a 2.5% transfer tax and a 1% stamp duty are payable when you sell real estate, calculated on the price or the improved value on the last land tax demand notice, whichever is higher.

There is also a 2% tax when you export foreign exchange.

Suzanne Davis
The purchase process – guidelines

In Barbados, once you sign an agreement to purchase real estate there is little room to withdraw if you change your mind, even if this is because you've made an unpleasant discovery about the property. There's a real risk you could lose your deposit if you can't or don't want to proceed with the purchase, and claiming compensation can be difficult or impossible. This is so even for very high-end properties, so it's best to be as informed as possible about the property before you agree to buy it.

With this in mind:

Don't sign anything without your lawyer reviewing it first.

You can commit yourself to buy an unsuitable property on unclear terms otherwise.

If you are corresponding with the vendor or his representatives, head all correspondence "subject to contract".

Letters and emails between yourself and the vendor or his agents can be a binding contract in some cases, and heading "subject to contract" prevents this happening prematurely.

Don't pay any money to anyone unless your lawyer advises it.

If you pay money prematurely, you could also be bound by a contract prematurely and on unsatisfactory terms. It might not be possible to get a refund if you can't or don't want to proceed when you have all the facts.

If you are borrowing, don't commit to a purchase until you have a written commitment for finance.

You need to know where the money to complete the purchase will come from before you commit to it, or you could lose your deposit if your loan isn't approved.

The time allowed for you to complete the purchase starts to run from the date you sign the sale agreement. So you could also run out of time under your sale agreement while waiting on financing, and again, lose your deposit as a result.

Carry out a thorough physical inspection of the property.
- Check for squatters, rights of way etc.
- Visit the property at different times of day and in different kinds of weather to see what it's like.
- Get an independent land surveyor to do a boundary certificate,

- which will tell you if there are encroachments onto the property or other problems on the ground. These may not show up in the deeds. Remember, the vendor's surveyor isn't independent – he doesn't work for you.
- Insist the contract says the line marks to the property are to be shown to you by a land surveyor.
- Vendors like to do this themselves to save cost, but you might be shown the wrong mark, or a mark that has been moved, or something that is not a mark at all.
- Ask to see any restrictive covenants applying to the property.

You need to be sure any covenants will not prohibit your using the property as you plan.

In newer developments covenants can be quite extensive, governing everything from the value and size of the buildings that can be constructed to the colour of the drapes that can be hung in the windows.

Check there is a legal right of way to access the property.

Does it allow trucks and commercial traffic, if you plan to develop the property, or use it for commercial purposes?

Find out if there are Homeowner's association levies or duties and how much they are.

What is the proposed completion date?

The vendor may need a quick or a long closing and you need to know if this works for you.

If the development is new, the vendor may insert an indefinite completion date, for instance: "30 days after the issue of a certificate of compliance". In these cases, you should ask for a provision to allow you to withdraw from the purchase and get back your deposit if the Vendor can't complete by a specified time.

Check the town planning status of the property.

It's important to know whether there are existing town planning violations. In Barbados if these have been in existence for over 4 years without action from the Town and Country Planning Department, no enforcement action can be taken. However, if violations exist and you want to develop the property later, correcting them may be a pre-condition of permission for your development.

Likewise, if there have been any refusals of planning permission in the past this may affect your planned development.

If you plan to develop the property you will also need to know what type of development will be permitted in the zone where the property is located. If the property is being sold "with planning permission" check to see if it's still valid – generally permissions have a 5-year life.

Remember also in Barbados changing how a property is used (from residential to offices, for instance) also requires planning permission.

Do note: having planning permission for a particular use does not mean that you won't be in breach of restrictive covenants. The two are completely separate issues. The Town Planning Department also does not consider rights of way when granting permission, so you must be sure you have a legal right of access over any road that town planning has designated as the property's access.

How do you want to own the property?

Will you be forming a company? Will it be local or overseas? Will you be sharing ownership with someone else? Decide on these things early and if you are using a company set it up in advance. If it's not a local company it must be registered in Barbados as an external company if it is to hold real estate here.

Why would I want to purchase the property through a company?

If the property is an investment, purchasing through a company may improve your tax position. While there are formation and maintenance costs for a company, these may be offset by advantages:
- You may be able to set off maintenance and operating expenses against income from the property, reducing the taxable income.
- It's a good way for more than one person in a business relationship to own property. Corporate documents provide structure as to the shares investors have in the investment, the

decision-making and management processes, and what happens if the investors disagree.
- Owning real estate through an overseas company may have tax advantages when you realize the investment.
- You should take tax advice both in your country of residence and in Barbados to see if this option is right for you.

Purchasing a building

In addition to all of the above:

Have the house fully inspected by the appropriate professionals before you commit to purchase.

Some of the professionals you should consider having inspect the building include (in addition to the land surveyor mentioned earlier):
- A civil engineer (checking soundness)
- An electrician (rewiring a house in Barbados can cost over US$15,000, and there can be a delay before it can be reconnected to the grid, as it must first be inspected by the Government Electrical Engineering Department)
- A plumber

Insure the building from the time you sign the purchase agreement

The risk of damage passes to the buyer from the time the sale agreement is signed. You will have to complete the purchase whether or not the building is damaged or destroyed.

You can adopt the vendor's insurance policy, but you cannot choose the terms and you won't know if there is anything that might make it void, so it may be better to have your own.

Check what's included

Does the vendor plan to remove air conditioners, built in appliances etc.?

Get a written inventory of everything that goes with the property and have it attached to the purchase agreement.

Purchase of a house "off plan".

An "off plan" purchase is a purchase of a building not yet constructed. There are differences for "off plan" purchases, because you are buying a building that does not yet exist. The purchase contract is a hybrid of a building contract and a purchase contract.

Are there detailed plans and specifications attached?

You should sign the plans and specs when you sign the contract and so should the vendor/builder.

Do the plans and specifications reflect what you expect to get?

The more detailed the specifications are, the better.

Plans should be approved by the Chief Town Planner.

Is the price firm?

If it is a fixed price contract, will it remain fixed if the price of materials goes up?

Is there a clear procedure for pricing and approving extras/variations?

This is the most common source of cost overruns in construction. Any extras or variations should be documented in writing, priced, and signed by both parties before they are carried out.

Is there a start date and an estimated completion date?

You do not want to be a party to the never-ending construction contract!

Is there is third party supervision?

A good building contract will have supervision by an independent architect or quantity surveyor built in.

Is there a snagging procedure, any retention of funds to give you security that snags and/or defects that occur on settling will be corrected, and what is the timetable for this?

Often, if you miss a deadline or do not follow the procedure set out, you may lose your opportunity to have any issues corrected.

What are the provisions regarding the builder's responsibilities?

Will he compensate you for late completion?

What happens if he goes bankrupt?

Who owns the materials bought with your money?
Can you sack the builder if you are not satisfied with progress?
What if he abandons the site?

Purchase of a company with real estate assets

If you are buying high end, commercial or development property, your purchase may be of holding company in which the underlying real estate asset is vested.

Your lawyers and accountants must then carry out due diligence on the company as well as the real estate.

Corporate due diligence can be extensive and complicated, if the company has been operating a business, or simple, where it only holds an asset.

You will need to know what the company's liabilities are, since you will be will be buying it with them, unless you get them discharged before.

Types of liabilities to consider include National Insurance, Value Added Tax, tax – corporation and otherwise, other debt and lawsuits

A purchaser should check all filings at the Companies' Registry are up to date, as the consequences of failing to file annual returns are significant (US$5.00 a day).

The Vendor should provide:
- Full details of bank accounts, auditors, assets etc.
- Financial statements
- Minute books
- Share registers
- Actual share certificates
- Company seals

If the company is an external company, there are two sets of due diligence, here in Barbados and in the country of incorporation.

Commercial properties

These may require heightened due diligence of the site, to ensure there are no chemical or biohazard contaminants from the last use of the property.

Buyers should also consider whether the use to which they want to put the property might cause a legal nuisance to the neighbours, because if it does, the neighbours may be able to obtain an injunction stopping the use, and possibly also damages.

Hotels, restaurants and similar properties require special licences to operate: to sell food or liquor, to allow the public use of a swimming pool and to host parties.

Steps in a purchase transaction

Checklist of documents includes:

Title Deeds - the vendor needs to provide these to your lawyer. I like to see copies of these before I negotiate the sale agreement, so if there is a problem I can deal with it in the contract.

Plans - should be recent – ideally not more than 20 years old.

Planning permissions.

National Insurance Clearance for the Vendor – eliminates the risk of a statutory charge over the property for any national insurance contributions the vendor may owe.

Land Tax certificate and land tax demand notice – producing these is a prerequisite to recording your conveyance (which transfers the property to you) at the Land Registry, and they also serve, as evidence there is no statutory charge over the property for unpaid land taxes.

Water bill and receipt – eliminates the risk of a statutory charge over the property for any unpaid water rates.

BRA Section 8A tax clearance certificate - required to record your conveyance at the Land Registry.

Incorporation Documents if you are buying a company, or buying from a company.

Letter of Intent to Sell/Offer to Purchase

A letter of intent to sell may be issued by a vendor or his real estate agent to a purchaser, offering to sell the property at a particular price.

The process might also begin with an offer to purchase issued by the purchaser or his lawyer.

It should always be issued subject to contract. This must be clearly stated, preferably at the head.

Reservation Agreement

Generally used in real estate developments, where the vendor wants to weed out all prospects that are not serious and the purchaser wants to get the property he's interested in off the market.

Check whether you will be able to get your reservation deposit back if after you have the facts you don't want to proceed.

Purchase and Sale Contract (Agreement for Sale)

These documents set out the terms and conditions of the sale and purchase – what is being bought, the price, the date for completion, how much the deposit is and who will hold it, any special considerations etc.

Your lawyer must review and negotiate the agreement for sale with the vendor's lawyer before you sign it. Bear in mind though, if you are buying into a new development the developer will be reluctant to allow many changes to the contract. If the purchasers don't all have the same "deal" the development becomes unmanageable.

Once you pay the deposit (usually 10%) and both parties have signed the agreement, you are committed to the purchase.

Investigation of title

This is the process by which your lawyer ensures you get what the vendor agreed to sell you.

Two types of title existing in Barbados simultaneously, and the way we investigate title differs for each.

Most of the land in Barbados falls under the unregistered system, which involves tracking the land from owner to owner, for at least 20 years (sometimes more). During this process any defects should be corrected. These can include inconsistent property descriptions, unprobated estates, missing deeds, release of previous mortgages etc.

A few areas in Barbados have been brought under the new registration of title system, which is a state run, and state backed system. Title investigation under this system should be simpler.

Conveyance/Transfer

This is the document that actually vests the title in your name. It is a highly specialized document that your lawyer will settle on your behalf.

How and when does completion take place?

Generally there is a period of three months after signing the agreement for sale before you are expected to complete the purchase, although this can vary from transaction to transaction. During this time the title will have been investigated, due diligence completed and the conveyance settled.

At closing, either there is a meeting where cheques are exchanged for documents, or documents and cheques are delivered in escrow.

The vendor provides utility transfer letters – you must take these to the utility provider after closing to get the accounts transferred to your name.

Land Tax is notified of the change of ownership as part of this procedure.

Neither you nor the vendor need be present at closing.

Your lawyer records the conveyance at the Land Registry, and when it is returned the deeds are handed to you (or the lender, if there is a mortgage, to be retained for the life of the loan).

Clarke Gittens Farmer is a commercial law firm, providing legal services for both domestic and international corporate and private clients. The firm has a reputation for high quality work in property, banking, corporate, commercial and business law areas. The firm is the Barbados member of Lex Mundi, the world's leading association of independent law firms.

Opportunity for High Net Worth Individuals- The Special Entry and Reside Permit
Dustin Delaney

The Special Entry and Reside Permit (SERP) was introduced by the Barbados Government in 2012 as a means of providing an opportunity for high net worth individuals (HNWIs) to obtain residency status on the island. The intention was to provide a credible, cost-effective means and user-friendly process by which HNWIs, their spouses and dependents are able to have protracted and less restricted access to Barbados. The aim of the SERP Programme was to build upon the existing platform of attracting HNWIs to the Barbados luxury lifestyle on a more permanent basis whilst affording them access to an environment of rational taxation. Unlike many of the Eastern Caribbean countries, Barbados does not sell citizenship and thus provides this as an alternative.

There are two qualifying SERP categories: (1) an investment in Barbados including a property investment of at least US$2 million from funds sourced outside Barbados along with evidence of net worth in excess of US$5 million (Category 1); and (2) an investment including a property investment of at least US$2 million from funds sourced outside of Barbados without evidence of net worth (Category 2). The Category 1 SERP allows for more opportunities.

"Investment" is defined to include rental real estate, property development projects, manufacturing, tourism, bank deposit, mutual funds or bonds, or any financial instrument. The broad scope certainly provides flexibility with respect to the types of investments that can be made. In fact, once could qualify for a SERP simply through the purchasing of a residence in Barbados, so long as the purchase price is at least $2 million. This in and of itself is a worthwhile investment on its own as the Barbados property market has proven to be one of the most resilient in the Caribbean.

There are no age restrictions per se for SERP applicants though they are granted based upon the category the individual falls within. This ranges from an indefinite period for those over 60 who are Category 1 applicants, to renewable five-year periods for Category 2 applicants no matter what age. Category 1 applicants under age 60 are able to renew the SERP and also obtain it indefinitely if certain criteria are met. The Category 1 SERP transitions to indefinite at age 60. Category 1 SERP holders are automatically entitled to work permits upon payment of a one time or per annum fee while Category 2 SERP holders are able to make an application for same.

Spouses and dependents of SERP holders are also eligible to obtain SERPs. Minors will be granted an automatic SERP until age eighteen and student visas are automatic during this period of time. Once over the age of eighteen, a dependent will be able to maintain the SERP so long as he/she is attending school and evidence to this effect needs to be produced every three years. Barbados boasts one of the highest literacy rates in the world and the island is well known for its sound education system, both public and private. Access to this is well sought after and products of this system test into top tier universities around the world. Spouses are eligible for work permits otherwise. The Barbadian social infrastructure is wide ranging and full of options.

The intention of the SERP was to have across the board appeal, in terms of attracting retirees, professionals of all ages, and those simply desiring the Barbados lifestyle offering. Barbados' reputation as the jewel of the Caribbean is internationally known and has long been a popular destination for HNWIs. Barbados is also an international business and financial services centre with an extensive network of bi-lateral investment and tax treaties, low tax rates, and a developed infrastructure. It has an expansive selection of vehicles and products for investment, insurance, and wealth management. This provides SERP holders the option of working from Barbados as many HNWIs have done so over the years.

SERP holders are able to establish tax residence in Barbados. Barbados is free of the burdens of capital gains, inheritance, and wealth taxes. Barbados also offers the foreign currency tax credit (FCTC). Persons resident but not domiciled in Barbados to be subject to tax on income derived in Barbados and income derived elsewhere but remitted to Barbados. Depending on the percentage of foreign currency earned in relation to the total earnings taxable in Barbados, the potential tax credit can amount to 93% of the income tax that would otherwise be payable in Barbados. In other words, it is possible to achieve an effective tax rate as low as 2.45% as to foreign sourced income brought to Barbados.

Whilst other governments in the region have decided to go the route of citizenship by investment, Barbados differentiated itself from its Caribbean counterparts in offering residence (including tax residence) specifically to cater to the HNWI. Barbados is one of a few paradises in the world that is able to satisfy the discerning HNWI. Moreover, a luxury Barbados property investment has proven to be a sound purchase as was seen during the recessionary period. The market continues to improve due in large part to the SERP that coincidentally has timed perfectly with the resurgence of the luxury real estate market in Barbados. This, complemented by the increasing demand for reasonable tax climates, has Barbados poised for continued growth as the SERP programme continues to garner recognition.

Dustin Delany of Delany Law is a Barbados based attorney at law practicing throughout the Commonwealth Caribbean. Delany Law is a client focused, result oriented practice premised upon first world standards. Mr. Delany is an international business law specialized focusing on investment throughout the region.

Conclusion

Wow!! I'm so excited about this little nugget of information on *Investing in Paradise*.

It was such an amazing experience writing this book on the A-Z of Real Estate in Barbados. I had all of this information stored up inside of me, which was accumulated over my 30 years of experience working in the industry. Once the tap was turned on, it came pouring out. In fact, once I got on a topic, more and more information kept coming, but I wanted to make sure that the book was short and concise; all the information that a buyer would need to make an informed decision on buying property in Barbados, and fun to read!

It was a great pleasure working with Daphne. She has become a wonderful friend and we make an excellent team as we are on the same wavelength.

I do hope that you have enjoyed reading my book and that it has answered all of your questions on purchasing property in Barbados.
Please feel free to view my website www.luxecaribbeanproperties.com or email Suzanne@luxecaribbeanproperties.com .

Suzanne

Printed in Great Britain
by Amazon